PASS

ME

ANOTHER

COASTER

For Carl & Angie -
Only the commas
are funny -

Dan

June 3, 2010 A.D.

PASS

ME

ANOTHER

COASTER

✳ ✳ ✳

daniel s. goodman

INFINITY
PUBLISHING

Copyright © 2010 by Daniel S. Goodman

ISBN 0-7414-5884-5

Printed in the United States of America

Published March 2010

INFINITY PUBLISHING
1094 New DeHaven Street, Suite 100
West Conshohocken, PA 19428-2713
Toll-free (877) BUY BOOK
Local Phone (610) 941-9999
Fax (610) 941-9959
Info@buybooksontheweb.com
www.buybooksontheweb.com

These pages are dedicated to

Malcolm Clark, for his technical support on this project and many others.

(why won't he mention the others? — mc)

I THANK THREE PALS

Joe Bauer, civil engineer and fellow bocce ball player, for his contributions to four of my previous books that include his graphic genius, cover designs, words of simple delight and constructive comments on *Pass Me Another Coaster*

and

Tim Chamberlain, a prominent music promoter and Bill Shine, the world's greatest living humorist for feeding me occasional off-beat one-liners for my looney tomes and one-man-shows.

WHY THE TITLE?

I compose 87.9% of my one-liners and musings on cocktail napkins and/or coasters at establishments where adult beverages are consumed by wonderful warm human beings in the Napa Valley.

Usually I scribble on these differently-shaped napkins and at a later date transcribe them into a computer and then immediately recycle them in a partially friendly environmentally green manner.

Recently, a mixologist buddy suggested that I neatly print my thoughts on said coasters — photograph them for inclusion in a book, titled,
PASS ME ANOTHER COASTER
I liked his idea...thank you, John Robison.

You'll note, however, not all my reflections are on coasters as some were a tiny, tiny, tiny, tiny bit too lengthy to fit.

Cheerio,

Me.

BILL OF FARE

* * *

I LIKE

Sexy giraffes
Mount Gay Rum
The "Big Band" era
Red Wing Shoes
Candy balloons and raspberries

I DISLIKE

Anchovies

The Pregnant Horse

Do woodpeckers
ever get headaches?

What did Yogi Berra mean

when he said,

"I'll catch up with you."

The Gorilla's Cage

*I wasn't always
      a stand-up comedian,*

but then I got hemorrhoids.

Bouchon

Did
Alexander Graham Bell
have phone-y
employees working
for him?

YOU GOTTA LOVE THE LAWS

on our nation's fine books regarding weed, especially when you read about 430,000 deaths per year from tobacco, 85,000 from alcohol, 7,500 from aspirin. I enjoy Mount Gay Rum, but I don't take aspirin anymore, not even baby aspirin. Hell, do I look like a baby?

Has anyone seen a person living in the street, dead with a joint in his or her hand?

I wonder if lawmakers know this is the 21st century.

DID YOU HEAR ABOUT THE YOUNG GUY

who was new to S&M? He was just learnng the ropes.

One of my favorite
five-syllable words

Hurley's
Yountville CA

impecunious

"THE GOODMAN"

Who would have thunk it - an adult beverage named after Yours Truly.

I'm a fan of Mount Gay Rum, and Bouchon, the popular bistro in Yountville, California, created a drink in my name with this rum as the main ingredient.

If you like rum, but won't be in Yountville soon, you can catch the recipe to the right.

Original recipe by John Robison.

Bouchon

The

Goodman

- *4-6 leaves Basil*
- *Muddle with 1/4 oz. lemon juice*
- *Splash simple syrup*
- *2 oz. Mount Gay Rum*
- *Finish with Fever Tree Ginger Ale*

Serve on the rocks.

The Pregnant Horse

Did Y.A. Tittle go to strip joints?

REGARDING MAJOR-LEAGUE BASEBALL,

do the San Francisco <u>Giants</u> have a problem hiring a <u>short</u>stop?

SOME CALLED IT SHEER CONCENTRATION

and others called it, *focus.* I think of it as:
Ben Hogan

NEVER LET IT BE SAID

that I didn't do my fair share of community service. Just think of the number of sunglasses and umbrellas I've left in public spaces.

WHEN THE CAB DRIVER

calls you the next morniing to see if you are
O.K., you know you had a good time.

MY FRIEND TIM WAS IN THE PRUNE BUSINESS

for many years and he knew several celebrities. He admits, while none of them bought prunes from his family company, he said they were still regular guys.

Was Dizzy Gillespie

Brix

light-headed?

THINGS THAT ARE NEAT
(IN HAIKU)

Cole Porter's lyrics
The musical, Guys And Dolls
Pitcher's perfect game

"Casablanca" movie script
Expiring in ecstasy
Sinatra's phrasing

Pure apricot juice
Small town egg salad sandwich
Off-the-wall sidekicks

THINGS NOT SO NEAT
(IN HAIKU)

Bosses who are pricks
Hecklers at comedy shows
Hangover from gin

Passing wind in crowds
Overly cutesy waiters
Tripping on shoelace

CARS HAVE FEELINGS TOO

When I was younger, I could distinguish one make of automobile from another. With few exceptions, I can't do that today. They are all jellybeans with different colors and the colors are nothing to write home about.

Why do auto czars outlaw styling? What's wrong with a little sex appeal? Cars have feelings too.

*A Man of Integrity
when we needed him-*

Brix

Walter Cronkite.

YOU GOTTA CHUCKLE

when Supreme Court nominees state at confirmation hearings that their personal reflections and/or philosophy do not enter into their decision-making process . . . that only the law dictates their vote.

Excuse me!

Who do they think they are kidding?

The gods will not look unkindly upon them if they look the whole world in the eye and confess they are of human origin and not robots fabricated on Planet Sesquipedalian in late fall.

In July 2009, Senator Dianne Feinstein of California neatly said at a confirmation hearing, "I do not believe that Supreme Court justices are merely umpires calling balls and strikes. Rather, I believe that they make the decisions as individuals who bring to the Court their own experiences and philosophies".

THE REASON I DIDN'T LIKE WILLIAM TELL,

he always played the same tune.

Bouchon

I love Aviation Gin

*Two shots of it
and you're flying.*

Politicians' Code Of Ethics

Brix

Don't get caught!

PORN FILMS ARE LIKE THE STOCK MARKET;

they both have their ups and downs.

IT'S CALLED DEMOCRACY

Dad asked his four boys, "O.K., who did it"?

None of them squealed, so he beat the hell out of all four.

THE BEST ADVICE I EVER RECEIVED FROM A STOCKBROKER

"Buy a stock low and sell it high and if it doesn't go up, don't buy it".

WHEN I MENTIONED TO MY HUMORIST FRIEND, BILL, THAT I WAS WORKING ON MY EIGHTH BOOK,

he replied, "You don't write books. You write pamphlets and they make good fly swatters".

Definition of a Machine

Brix

Tiger Woods

*I'm not sure
I buy into the thought*

*that wisdom is the product
of age. but you'll find few
philosophers in a nursery.*

Every time I buy you chips

TRAVIGNE
NAPA VALLEY

they end up on your shoulders.

S.H.I.T.

"Thank God it's Friday" (T.G.I.F.) is a popular phrase among the esoteric and the non-esoteric, but I opt for the less often spoken line, "So happy it's Thursday". It has a more positive ring to it.

If you don't mind small change, you may like the parody to the right. The original lyrics are shown below.

PENNIES FROM HEAVEN

Ev'ry time it rains, it rains pennies from heaven
Don'tcha know each cloud contains pennies from heaven?
You'll find your fortune fallin' all over town
Be sure that your umbrella
Is upside down

Trade them for a package of sunshine and flowers
If you want the things you love, you must have showers
So when you hear it thunder
Don't run under a tree
There'll be pennies from heaven for you and me

PARODY ON
PENNIES FROM HEAVEN

Ev'ry time it pains I drink at Seven Eleven;
Don'tcha know my honour stains at Seven Eleven?
You'll find my reputation bad all over town;
Be sure your friends are faithful
To your renown.

Trade your booze for dozens of tall whisky sours;
If you drink the drink you love, you must have
  sours.
So when an evening is boring,
Don't come complaining to me;
There'll be drinks at Seven Eleven for free.

Just curious

1. Are cucumber festivals seedy?

Hurley's
Yountville CA

2. Are guacamole tastngs
morale boosteers?

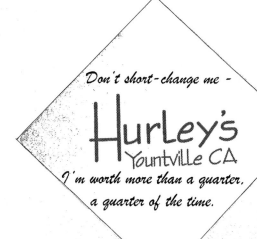

Don't short-change me -

Hurley's
Yountville CA

I'm worth more than a quarter,
a quarter of the time.

Sorry, no place bet!

The Gorilla's Cage

I had an uncle
who was so conservative,

he wouldn't make a place bet
on a match race.

Bouchon

How Canned Laughter
Got Started

———

A member of the audience threw
tomatoes at a vaudeville performer
and didn't take them out of
the can.

I AM NOT AN ADVOCATE

of teachers passing out hours of homework to kids. I think it's the teachers' duty to enlighten the students for the time they spend in the classroom and not burden them with hours of homework.

What's wrong with kids playing sports after school, enjoying the arts, rapping with their friends or sucking up on an ice cream soda versus slaving away over math problems or composing an essay...

IN THE SHOW-BUSINESS ARENA,

I like what Eddy Cantor said, "Likeabiity is 90% of the battle."

I OFTEN DO ONE-MAN SHOWS WHEN I OUTNUMBER THE AUDIENCE

and that's neat as I don't have to deal with hecklers.

If you're a fan of the motion picture, **Casablanca**, don't overlook the parody to the right. The original lyrics are below.

AS TIME GOES BY

You must remember this, a kiss is still a kiss,
A sigh is just a sigh, the fundamental things apply,
As time goes by . . .

An' when two lovers woo, they still say "I love you,"
On that you can rely, no matter what the future brings,
As time goes by . . .

Moonlight an' love songs never out of date,
Hearts full of passion, jealousy an' hate,
Woman needs man and man must have his mate,
That no one can deny . . .

It's still the same old story, a fight for love an' glory,
A case of do or die, the world will always welcome lovers,
As time goes by . . .

It's still the same old story, a fight for love an' glory,
A case of do or die, the world will always welcome lovers,
As time goes by . . .

PARODY ON *AS TIME GOES BY*

You must remember this —
A miss is just a miss,
A bye is just a bye;
You'll never get it past the net
When all balls fly.

And when your golfing swing
Sends your ball up on the wing
Way up there in the sky,
No matter how the skylark sings
When all balls fly.

Under the starlight
Down by Lover's Lane;
Caught in the carlight
With a girl called Jane.
She just needs you
And you don't feel just pain —
That no one can deny.

Well, it's still the same old story,
A fight for sex that's hoary,
A case of scotch or rye;
The world will always welcome plovers
When all balls fly.

**HE APPEARED IN JUST A FEW
MOTION PICTURES — ALL TALKIES,
BUT BOY, COULD HE STEAL A
SCENE WITHOUT SPEAKING A
WORD!**

Movie buffs know him as James Dean.

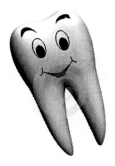

I TOLD MY REGULAR DENTIST

I used to be in the military. He said, "I used to be a drill sergeant."

WHAT'S THE BIG DEAL

about engraving dates of one's birth and death onto a tombstone —

Hell, most persons are not aware of when they are born and when they die; so why not list significant dates on their tombstones that they were aware of, e.g. the first time they sewed wild oats and the number of times they were arrested.

IT'S MY ALL RED SALAD

If Red is not one of your favorite colors, please do not read any further.

This is a salad prepared with all red colored vegetables that I developed all by my lonesome when I was with six wonderful warm human beings in early evening -one day in mid-Spring of the year 2006 A.D. at a private gathering in Napa Valley, California. U.S.A., Western Hemisphere, Planet Earth, Milky Way Galaxy.

Since then, friends and acquaintances in the culinary arena (culinary-that's a sumptuous four syllable word) got wind of the dish (actually, not the dish, just the salad) and served it on dishes at catered affairs and occasionally included it on their restaurant's fare. One salad buff said. "It's better than sex on Thursdays". Do you think he was kidding???

If you do not have anything better to do now, review the following recipe. If you can't make the time to digest (digest-that's not a bad word relating to food) this narrative recipe, not to worry. After all, this book is dedicated mostly to brevity, in fact, Martha C. Brevity and not to narrative, as in, Sydney P. Narrative.

Now to the facts of the case, or put another way ... "Let's get started".

Take two bunches of red radishes. Clean them with loving care. Separate them. Cut them in circles not too thick, now. Then put them in a bowl of cold water and place in the refrigerator for at least 64 minutes. That wasn't too bad.

Next...clean with alacrity two red bell peppers. Cut them into 1/4 inch width squares.

Place in a bowl of cold water and put into the refrigerator. If you are so inclined, you may

place the cut red peppers with thoughtfulness into the same bowl that currently holds the cut radishes. Leave in refrigerator for at least 54 minutes.

Are you getting tired or are you ready to go on. This will all end soon (hopefully).

Where was I before I so rudely interrupted myself? Oh yes, the recipe.

Take twelve baby beets that are steamed and peeled and place on your cutting board, (I like that sentence). Cut into eighths. Put into a bowl and momentarily set aside within seven or eight inches from your cherished cutting board.

Next...get eight or nine romaine tomatoes. Don't forget to wash them. Cut them lengthwise in quarters. Neatly place them in the same bowl as the beets, as you may remember, are currently seven or eight inches

from your cutting board. Do not mix or toss them together at this specific moment in time.

Get yourself 1/2 pound baby shrimp, cooked, of course. Just leave the package in the refrigerator for now. It won't be lonesome. It has fabulous company.

Granted, this is called a red salad, but I like to add an item that is not red in color and that item is known as Jarlsberg Cheese. I *love* (yes, <u>love</u>-not just, like) its color, its texture, its flavor more than I do my ninth cousin and, in my humble opinion, it makes for a glorious complement to this concoction. Cut this gorgeous chunk of cheese into 1/4 inch squares. The idea here is not to make the pieces too thick, but just thick enough. You'll know when it is right. Just get into it. Let it flow. It's all about the FLOW (FLOW? I wonder if that would make a good name for a soap product.

Call me nuts if you will, but just watch some soap manufacturer adapt the name). Store the cut cheese in the frig and cover it with tender care.

Approximately, but not less than 18.37 minutes before serving, remove all contents from the frig. Place all the veggies (some might call the tomatoes a fruit) in a large salad bowl. Don't forget to first drain the water from the radishes and the peppers. (Betcha the radishes and peppers are nice and crisp now). Neatly mix all the ingredients. Once mixed to your satisfaction, you can add a touch or two or three of a red-colored dressing as, *Catalina*, and slightly toss. You do not want to overdo it. You don't want it to be soup-like or mushy. The gods wouldn't like that.

I can't tell you with judicious uncertainty how many homo sapiens this divine succulent

product that you just created will serve. On that score, the ball is in your court. For instance, what size are your salad bowls? Are you just serving buffet style? Many factors will enter into your top management-making process.

If you do serve the salad in bowls, may I suggest placing on the top of each salad, 1/2 hard cooked egg and a couple slices of avocado. That would be neat.

You might send a sampling to Popeye if he's still not stuck on just one vegetable.

Well, that wasn't all that bad—only six pages of narrative for the *RED* at heart.

Happy serving!

I HAVE A QUESTION

Do podiatrists have ingrown personalities?

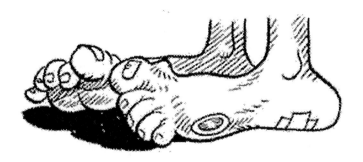

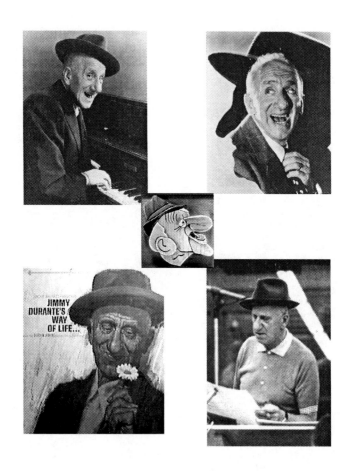

HE SOLD BOTH THE SIZZLE
AND THE STEAK

- A beloved star of vaudeville
- A pianist
- He was a comedian revered for his comic language butchery
- He was a singer with a distinctive gravel delivery
- An actor
- A television and movie icon
- A radio star
- A bandleader
- He was a nightclub entertainer
- He was a songwriter
- He was Mister Showman who sold both the sizzle and the steak
- He was Durante, Jimmy, that is

Note: Durante recorded a multitude of songs— *As Time Goes By*, *Make Someone Happy*, and *Umbriago* were a few of his many hits.

My favorite, however, was his rendition of *Old Man Time*. I recited it in one of my One-Man Shows. It's a moving number. Look it up.

The Goodman-II
(not the cocktail — the author)

Crapper Dan

There was an author named Dan
Who wrote as he sat on the can;
It made him so happy
To write such things crappy
That now he has only one fan.

Several following pages briefly describe the bars and restaurants celebrated in this tome.

BOUCHON

6534 Washington Street
Yountville, California
94599

In the traditiional, relaxed atmosphere of a French bouchon, guests are welcome in the dining room, at the outdoor cafe tables or at the zinc bar. Dining can be as simple as a plate of oysters and a glass of wine, a cappuccino and a lemon tart, or as elaborate as a full course dinner paired with outstandiing wines.

BRIX

7377 Saint Helena Highway
Yountville, California
94558

Located on Highway 29 a few minutes drive north of Yountville, California, Brix Restaurant and Gardens is an entirely new incarnation of the wine-country classic with focus on farm-to-table dining. Brix is designed to take full advantage of its 16 prime Napa Valley acres that have given the restaurant an entirely new look and feel.

Brix's patio and garden vineyard area are both popular venues for private events.

THE CAGED GORILLA

On a Monkeyside Road off Highway 29, half way from Yountville to Saint Helena.

Outer walls bright red, door large enough to pass a Neanderthal, quiet desperation inside. At the far end of the bar stands a stuffed gorilla. He holds a big cage inside which is the remnant of a man.

Some have gone <u>ape</u> over their signature drink, **The Gorilla Fizz**.

Strangely, drinks are not free.

COMPADRES RIO GRILLE

505 Lincoln Avenue
Napa, California
94558

Located on the Napa River, Compadres is a favorite with locals that serves Western food with a Mexican accent and has a full bar.

Their summer Sunday afternoon Music-By-The-River Series on the wraparound deck is a big hit.

HURLEY'S

6518 Washington Street
Yountville, California
94599

All-day seasonal fare, seven days a week, emphasizing fresh local ingredients.

Patio and lively bar.

Their great Wild Game Week in November is a welcome event with the locals and tourists alike.

Private dining room for parties.

Walking distance to local hotels.

The Pregnant Horse

The Pregnant Horse is an old-style tavern on Mule Lane, just off highway 29 between Yountville and St. Helena, California.

The price range is reported to be ridiculous. It accepts no credit cards.

Parking on the street if you can find it, wheelchair accessible, outdoor lounging, indoor scrounging.

Juke box music, slink in on Friday Saturday, Sunday nights.

No happy hour, you'll be happy full time. The Pregnant Horse's signature drink is
The Equestrian Shot.

Tra Vigne

1050 Charter Oak Avenue
Saint Helena, California
94574

Across the railroad tracks from Highway 29 in Saint Helena (the Wine Train from Napa comes by four times per day).

Quiet garden (except for moments at train time), large outdoor eating area where grooms unwisely marry brides about once a week.

Inside, a discreet atmosphere, fine menu, comfortable bar and strangely decorated with large paintings (e.g. a monkey drinking from a bottle).

AND IN CONCLUSION

It's really been a pleasure
and a lot of fun.
Thanks to my readers
each and every one.

To my friends,
my supporters,
my relatives,
my favorite enemies--
the short, the fat, the tall.
I hope that covers everyone.

That's all!

Thank you, Sarah, for your eternal love.

ABOUT THE AUTHOR

From buffoon, to actor, to hambone Hamlet, to logistician, to gold medalist freestyle swimmer, real estate broker, raconteur, insurance agent, veteran, tournament caliber table-tennis player, character model, poet, award winning principal performer in TV and radio commercials, production control, the culinary arena, the sewn products industry, polyethylene products, assignment in the Arctic to desert duty, to horseplayer, Daniel S. Goodman has traveled in a curious sphere of diversity.

Visit Dan's cool website, winsomedan.com. It exudes hilarity with dignified indignance.

———————

Among Dan's multifarious attributes is that of a lyricist and you can download Dan's songs on some 16 Internet music stores under the album name, **Devil And A Tease**. He's got some neat lyrics, especially the songs, **Devil And A Tease**, **Still**, and **Toes And Turtles, Tigers I Like**.

———————

By the time this book goes to press, Dan's two comedy albums,
Nonsense In The Key Of Z-Flat
and
So You Think You Have A Problem
should be available to download on several intenet comedy stores. He's a hoot!

NOTES TO MYSELF

NOTES TO OTHERS

FINAL NOTE